THE IMPACT OF WORLD

THE SMESTOW VALE

CU00746774

THE IMPACT OF WORLD WAR ONE ON

THE SMESTOW VALE VILLAGES

DAVID TAYLOR

YOUCAXTON PUBLICATIONS

OXFORD & SHREWSBURY

ISBN 978-1-911175-74-2
Printed and bound in Great Britain.
Published by YouCaxton Publications 2017

YouCaxton Publications
enquiries@youcaxton.co.uk

Contents

Introduction

This pamphlet tells the story of the impact of World War One on the South Staffordshire villages of Smestow Vale, Bobbington, Himley, Swindon, Trysull, Seisdon and Wombourne. It is hoped that it gives some indication of what was happening back at home whilst the fighting took place in France and elsewhere. No history of World War One can ignore the impact of millions of men enlisting and leaving their homes to go to war and that is where this history will start.

102 men from these seven villages have been identified as having served in the First War. Seventy-three were identified from the various memorials preserved in the villages and twenty-nine from searches through military records. Of the 102 seventy-four died, only twenty-eight survived. The relatively low level of survivors reflects the loss of many of these records over time, especially due to bombing during World War Two, as well as the difficulty of tracing people who migrated out of the area.[1] As discussed in more detail later, throughout much of the nineteenth and early twentieth centuries, this area of South Staffordshire experienced high levels of net out-migration. By including both deaths and survivors, a rounder picture of the impact of the war can be gleaned. Parish and Rural District council minutes and papers provide a valuable insight into the social concerns of the period, especially on housing but also on other, more mundane topics such as the bus service to Wombourne and the telephone service across Smestow Vale. Local papers are often

---

[1] See ancestry.co.uk description of the World War One UK Military Records for more information.

a good source of information but unfortunately, Smestow Vale is not served with its own newspaper and the parishes we are concerned with very rarely appeared in the newspapers of, for example, Wolverhampton. However church records, especially the register of services and vestry -meeting minutes, did illuminate some of the various parish activities. The title of a sermon can also help us to discern the attitudes of the preacher and the different types of social pressure the congregations were subject to.

The final section of this pamphlet looks very briefly at various topics where few or no written references have been found in the local archives. The author would be very pleased to receive further information on these and any other related subjects.

The Armed Forces

JOINING UP

It is known that motivations for enlisting were varied. There was a general belief for many years that war with Germany was very likely and this was reflected in novels such as *The Invasion of 1910* by William Le Queux, published in 1906, which is typical of the genre.[2] The general message from nearly every authority - state, school, church and newspapers -emphasised the need to serve King and Country and to help the 'plucky' Belgians whose country was 'being raped'. Whilst peer pressure was often referred to in many cases, this is better understood in the sense of a group of friends deciding to enlist together. For some, enlistment was seen as an adventure or as an opportunity to escape a dull life for men who might have enjoyed a taste of army life in territorial summer camps. For others, enlistment could be an economic opportunity or an option that allowed them to 'get one over' on an unpopular employer.

For many, enlistment was an impromptu decision, made as they passed a recruiting meeting but for others it was not always a spur-of-the-moment action, indicating that it came about from a mixture of motives and that men also experienced pressures not to enlist. Unfortunately, we only have one personal record from one of the village men, private William Frederick Jones, describing why he joined up, so we can only assume what factors were most relevant for the rest of them.

---

2   Le Queux, William, *The Invasion Of 1910*, Eveleigh Nash, 1906. Chapter 1 describes a surprise German invasion of eastern England.

The Attestation Form, or signing up paper for Private Joseph Thomas Lawley, an oath that he will serve for the 'duration of the war' and that he 'will be faithful and bear true allegiance to His Majesty King George the Fifth'.

William Herbert Ison originally enlisted on 28th January 1909 when he was just seventeen. Since 1908, the lower age limit for the regular army was eighteen but for the territorial army it was seventeen, so he enlisted for six years' service almost as soon as it was legally possible. Following his eighteenth birthday in 1910, he signed his papers for the regular army and joined the Welsh Regiment, spending some time in Wales and in India. However, army life did not seem to suit him and he faced various disciplinary charges, including 'Attempting to obtain beer after hours, using obscene language to an NCO and striking a civilian'. It was no surprise therefore, that he managed to find enough money - £18 - to purchase his discharge on 13th January 1914. However, thirteen days after war was declared by Britain he enlisted again, this time with the South Staffordshire Regiment. An advert appeared in the Express and Star in August 1914 asking directly for 'Trained Men' to re-join the 6th South Staffordshire Territorial battalion and as a trained infantryman with recent army experience and aged only twenty-two, he was in the first group to be targeted for recruitment; he would also have been subject to peer and societal pressure to fulfil his duty to his country.

Though William appears not to have re-enlisted due to economic pressures, giving his employment on re-joining as a turner for the Sunbeam Motor Car Company, it may well be an economic indicator that of the eighty-five men whose pre-1914 occupation is known, fourteen were already in the army (a significantly higher proportion than average of the British male population, which in 1911 was 19.7 million, while the regular army numbered only about 245,000[3]); twenty-five were

---

3   Tucker, Spencer; Roberts, Priscilla Mary, *World War I: Encyclopedia*, 2005, p 504.

farm workers which was then a lowly paid occupation, making it likely that joining up had the attraction of much better pay and conditions.

Pressure from the church to enlist was certainly the subject of sermons preached at Sunday services. The Reverend Edmund Parry Nicholes, at St Benedict Biscop in Wombourne, preached on 'The war - intercession for help', taking Exodus chapter 17 verse 11 as his text. Presumably his message was that God would intervene in this war in a similar way to that which he did in the passage, where while Moses' hands were held aloft, the Israelites were winning. He delivered a less subtle message in August, when he took the text Matthew chapter 8 verse 9, with the title 'The centurion's Servant'. This passage is usually used to illustrate the faith of the centurion but here, the Reverend Nicholes concentrated on the centurion's servant, who was obedient to the command of his master: little needs to be added here to see the endorsement for the call to serve. Whilst the Reverend Nicholes could be subtle, the Reverend John Wilson Andrews at Trysull was nearly always more straightforward in his choice of text and title. On 2nd August, even before war had been officially declared, he chose Proverbs chapter 29 verse 10; 'The bloodthirsty hate the upright: but the just seek his soul'. On 9th August, his text was Psalm 144 verses 1 and 2, 'Blessed be the Lord my strength, which teacheth my hands to war and my fingers to fight: My goodness and my fortress; my high tower and my deliverer; my shield and he in whom I trust; who subdueth my people under me.'. His sermons through the rest of 1914 continued in a similar vein.[4]

There is little evidence of friends enlisting in groups together, which is perhaps not surprising, as there was only one large single employer in the vale, the ironworks at Swindon, which employed

---

4   D5841/2/1 – Wombourne St Benedict Register of Services and D3452/2/4
    – Trysull All Saints Register of Services: Staffordshire Archives.

about 150 people. The biggest single occupation was farm work which was highly dispersed, giving fewer opportunities for work colleagues to sign up. Of the thirty-seven people for whom we have military records, there are no duplicate dates for enlisting and only four that are within a day of each other. Rather than a spur -of -the moment decision, the ages of these men at enlistment suggests that there had been some consideration. Only eight of the men were under twenty, with nineteen aged between twenty and twenty-nine, while eight were over thirty, with the oldest being forty-six. Similarly, compulsory service seems to have had little overall impact. Almost two thirds of those who enlisted, did so before conscription was introduced in March 1916. The average age at enlistment before and after March 1916, only increased by just over two years from twenty-two to twenty-four. Perhaps a more telling statistic is the number of enlistments per month; 1.1 before and 0.4 after this date, indicating that the pool of available men had been pretty well emptied before conscription was introduced.

The diaries of William Frederick Jones, and the reminiscences of his daughter May Griffiths, show that he volunteered on 15th September 1914, giving a somewhat enigmatic reason; he had no wife or children and 'He should go'. Perhaps this simple phrase reflects some of the sense of community and duty that existed at the time.[5]

THOSE WHO DIED

The most obvious source of information is provided by the various memorials and obelisks in the graveyards at St Benedict Biscop in Wombourne and All Saints in Trysull, the plaques in St John the Evangelist in Swindon, St Michael in Himley and

---

5 *One Soldier One War*, C.53, Wombourne And District Local History Room, p.10.

Holy Cross in Bobbington, as well as the stained glass window in the United Reformed Church in Wombourne. These record information on those 'Who gave their lives for their country', usually including name, rank, battalion and regiment. Seventy-three men are named, but reviewing the military records, one, Rifleman Alfred Rogers, who died in service on 15th August 1916, was also found but is not included on any of the memorials, making a total of seventy- four known deaths of Smestow Vale men.

This raises the question of why Alfred Rogers is not recorded. At his baptism at St Benedict Biscop on 5th March 1894, there is no mention of a father, while his mother Martha Jane Guest, is named as a single woman. In the census of 1901, he is living with his mother, grandparents and other members of the extended family in Rookery Lane, Wombourne. In the 1911 census he is still living with his grandparents in Wombourne, which is also designated as his birthplace. Military records show Mr E. Rogers as his next of kin, living in Rookery Lane in August 1919 and as burial records show that E. Rogers was not buried until 1927, it is likely that Alfred's next of kin was still in the village at the time the memorial was being created. It is possible that he was not included on the memorial because he died of pneumonia rather than war wounds.

As well as one person apparently left off the memorials there is one other who was duplicated; William Richard Millward is named on both the Trysull and Himley memorials, perhaps because in both the 1901 and 1911 censuses he was living with his uncle in Trysull while his father lived in Himley. Possibly they both put his name forward when the memorials were compiled. It was not unusual for an individual to be named on more than one memorial, as they were erected by a diverse range of organisations. Captain Sydney John Sankey was recorded on the Wombourne memorial, where the family were living at the time and in Bilston, on his father's firm's memorial. Lieutenant Leslie Gardner Shaw, who was on the Queen Street Congregational Church's memorial in Wolverhampton, is also remembered by a window at the United Reformed Church in Wombourne, because of a close family tie to the Wombourne church, even though they lived some distance away to the west of Wolverhampton (Leslie Shaw's grandfather, John Shaw, laid the foundation stone of the Wolverhampton church on 7th October 1850 and the family remained a major benefactor to the church.)

[Left] Lieutenant Shaw whose death was commemorated at Queen Street, Wolverhampton, and Wombourne United Reformed Church memorials (Wolverhampton Archive File). [Right] Captain Sankey whose death was commemorated at the Sankey factory and Wombourne memorials.

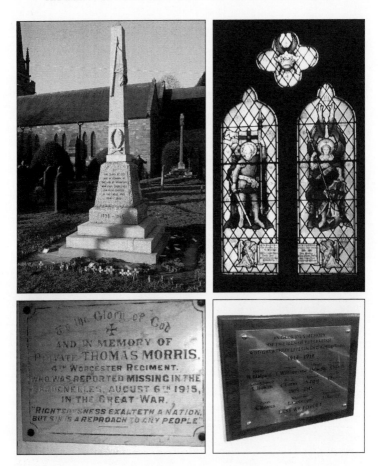

[Top left] Wombourne's Memorial. [Top right] Swindon's Window.
[Bottom left] Bobbington's Plaque. [Bottom right] Swindon's Plaque.

Approximately half of these men were in the South Staffordshire Regiment, while the remainder were in a wide range of other regiments and corps. Infantry regiments predominated, with sixty-one of the total seventy-four; four were in the Royal Artillery, one in the Machine Gun Corps, one on HMS Agincourt, one in the Royal Flying Corps, with no information available on the remaining six.

Trysull's Plaque and Memorial

Their deaths ranged across most of the major campaigns on
the Western Front, from the 'Race for the coast' in the autumn of
1914, the Second Battle of Ypres and the Battle of Loos in 1915.
Five died at Delville Wood during the Battle of the Somme in
1916, which was also the year of the Easter Irish Rebellion, where
one Wombourne soldier was killed.

In 1917 a series of battles and actions culminated with the
First Battle of Passchendaele and the Battle of Cambrai at the
end of the year. The Battle of Cambrai was notable as the first
successful 'all arms' operation, showing that the lessons on how to
use modern weapons together to overcome the German defences
on the Western Front had been learnt, not only at Corps and Army
levels, but all the way down to company and platoon. Smestow
Vale men were involved in many of these actions and battles from
Private John Munday on 28th January to Private Thomas Nichols
on 14th December.

In the Spring of 1918, following Haig's famous 'Backs to the
wall' communication on 11th April, the Germans began to lose
momentum, suffering the same problems earlier experienced by

[Left] Himley's Plaque. [Right] Wombourne URC's Window.

the Western Allies in their large scale offences. The successes of the battles of Bapaume and Havrincourt in August and September 1918, proved that Haig's armies had mastered the techniques and tactics needed to defeat the Germans in their heavily defended positions of the Hindenburg Line. During the following months, two other factors helped in Germany's defeat; large numbers of American units took up position on the front line and the German soldier's willingness to fight was declining. The decisive Allied victories in 1918, from the first Battle of Bapaume in March, to those of Epehy, Saint Quinton Canal and Selle in September and October, which all saw men from the Vale die, finally convinced the German commanders and civilians that all was lost and led to the request for an Armistice.

Even when there were no set-piece battles, local actions including trench raiding, artillery and mortar fire and snipers made the front a dangerous place at any time. Private T Clinton

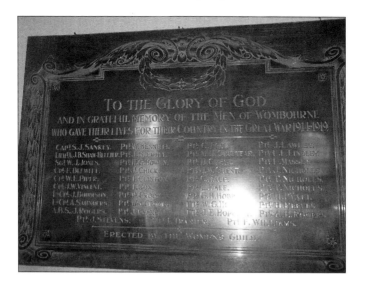

Wombourne URC's Plaque.

of the 10th Battalion, West Yorkshire Regiment (Prince of Wales's Own) died of wounds on 14th November 1915 when his division, which had landed in France in July 1915, undertook trench familiarisation and then held a 'quiet' line in the southern area of the Ypres Salient. Disease and accidents were also a hazard; Gunner George Henry Malpass is recorded as having 'Died of disease' and Private John Munday died of pneumonia.

For the wounded, death could occur sometime after the battle: Private Charles Corns of the 7th Battalion South Staffordshire Regiment was discharged in July 1916 after being wounded at Gallipoli. He died on 15th January 1918 but at this distance, with no documentary evidence, it is impossible to say if this was due to the effect of his wounds. At the time there was obviously some debate as to his level of disability and he was subject to a number of medical boards to determine his pension. On 30th October 1917, a doctor wrote that 'He is a cripple and unable to

Officers of 'B' Company, 1st/6th Battalion, South Staffordshire Regiment in No.38 Trench, Hill 60, three miles south-east of Ypres during March 1915. Left to right: Lieutenant Walter Nelson, Major Edwin Lewis, Lieutenant Gerald Howard Smith. Walter Nelson's death seven months later is commemorated on the Trysull memorial. Imperial War Museum image Q60504.

get about' and stated that even if he was 'otherwise healthy', the damage to the eye that he suffered in Gallipoli would still make him '50%' disabled.

The last of the Vale deaths to be recorded on the Western Front were Private James Thomas Boddison, of the 1st/5th Battalion, South Staffordshire Regiment and Private John Stevens of the 1st/6th (T.F.) Battalion, South Staffordshire Regiment, who both died, three days apart in the battle for Saint Quintin Canal. From Swindon, Private Alex James Piper, also of the 1st/6th Battalion, South Staffordshire Regiment, died at Selle on the 19th October 1918, in one of the battles following the breach of the Hindenburg Line. Six days later, Private Samuel Edward Wilkes in the 18th Brigade of the Royal Field Artillery, who was from

Himley, died in the Final Advance in Artois. At the time, neither they nor anyone else on the Allied side realised how close to the end of the war they were. Deaths continued after the Armistice on 11th November 1918; Private J. W. Guest, from the 3rd Battalion, Sherwood Foresters (Notts and Derby Regiment) and the Labour Corps, died on Tuesday 8th April 1919, aged forty, at the Military Hospital, Whittington, Lichfield.

Men from the Vale served and died in other places as well as the Western Front. Four were killed in Gallipoli; Private Ernest Victor Starkey Pedley from Trysull, attached to the 11th Battalion of the Australian Imperial Force, died on 6th August and on the same day, Private Thomas Morris, from Bobbington died whilst serving with the 4th Battalion the Worcestershire Regiment. Two days later Private Thomas Baker from Himley, serving with the 7th Battalion of the South Staffordshire Regiment, was killed and finally, Lt. Arthur Joseph Bradney Shaw-Hellier, also of the 7th Battalion, died on the 9th August 1915. These units were part of the 11th (Northern) Division, which had landed on 6th – 7th August. They had faced the Turks for no more than three days. Fighting was harsh and hard in that campaign.

The Royal Navy is represented by Ordinary Seaman John Rogers, on HMS Agincourt, who died aged eighteen, on 2nd September 1917 and was buried at Dalmeny and Queensferry Cemetery, West Lothian. The story of HMS Agincourt is one of the more unusual in the Royal Navy; the keel was laid by British Armstrong Whitworth, for an order from the Brazilian navy in 1911, for a ship to be called the Rio de Janeiro. At the time, Brazil was in an arms race with Argentina and with a booming economy, ordered the building of the largest dreadnought in the world, with fourteen heavy guns in seven turrets. Unfortunately, Brazil's economy was heavily dependent on coffee and when the international price of coffee fell, Brazil could not pay for the ship. The Turks then stepped in and bought it, with a scheduled completion in 1914 but when the war broke out, the War Office impounded the ship, renaming her HMS Agincourt. She appears to have only been engaged in one action, in Jutland in 1916. Her armament was considered much too thin for her to be a front line ship and she was retired in 1919 and scrapped in 1922.

The Royal Flying Corps, predecessor to the Royal Air Force, is represented by two people, one more obliquely than the other. Kevin Robert Furniss from Trysull, was a lieutenant in the 23rd Squadron: his military career is fairly typical for those who served in the Royal Flying Corps because he was originally in the Staffordshire Yeomanry and transferred as the new corps was developed. He was from an educated background, his father being an electrical and mechanical engineer; he was also young, being only nineteen when he died on 29th April 1917. The other was Alfred Charles Bindschadler, who enlisted in July 1918, at the relatively old age of forty-one. His civilian occupation was master of the Seisdon Workhouse, so again, an educated man. He applied to join the newly formed Royal Air Force but was turned down and instead served in the Royal Army Service Corps as a Horse Transport Driver.

One little -remembered but interesting operation is marked in the death of Private John Thomas Wharton from Trysull, who died in July 1917 whilst serving with the 1st Battalion of the Loyal North Lancashire Regiment. Military commanders were very concerned about how to break *through*, not just *into* the German defences. One line of thought which had been considered since 1915, was to go around the defences by a sea-borne invasion of the Belgian coast north of the German lines at Yser, to be coordinated with major offensives around the Ypres Salient. This sea-borne offensive was called Operation Hush. The Germans, are thought to have recognised the danger and launched a counter-offensive, called Operation Strandfest on 10th July, using mustard gas for the first time. After much fighting in July and August, the British offensive was cancelled.

Only five of the seventy-four are buried in Smestow Vale cemeteries, having died of wounds, accidents or disease in England. The remaining sixty-nine lie on or near the battlefields where they died, though many of the bodies were never found, especially those who died on a battlefield that was fought over many times in the course of the war. We know exactly where those who died in an overseas hospital, such as Private William Henry Walker from Trysull, are buried. The casualty station or hospital would use a local piece of land as a cemetery if there was not already an adequate facility. Private Walker suffered a gun-shot wound (GSW) to the leg, was admitted to hospital on 20th October 1916, and died at 3:35am the following day.

THOSE WHO SERVED AND RETURNED
IDENTIFYING THEM

It is not easy to discover just how many men from these villages served in the armed forces during the war. Many of the military records were destroyed in World War Two, were lost or disposed of over time, or are now unreadable due to bad storage conditions; search terms such as 'Wombourne' in the surviving records, identified only twenty-seven men from ancestry.co.uk. Added to this is Private William Frederick Jones, whose wartime diaries are preserved in Wombourne Library's history archive.[6] To

---

6   *One Soldier One War.*

check how complete this result was, all those recorded on the war memorials were also searched for but out of seventy-three, only seven were found; approximately 10%, suggesting that possibly as many as 270 men from the Vale served and returned. This is partially confirmed by Wombourne Parish Council's minutes, stating that 140 men would be attending 'A dinner for men who had served in the war', even though only sixteen have been positively identified.[7] We can assume that this number would have included councillors and other dignitaries who were welcoming the men back. Therefore, in broad terms, we can estimate that perhaps 120 men from Wombourne saw active service in the war and then returned to Britain, indicating that this search has uncovered only about 13% of the total.

THEIR SERVICE EXPERIENCE

Three had already enlisted, either in 1912 or 1913, before the war began, while the last recruits were Private Joseph Cox, in May 1917 and Private Alfred Charles Bindschadler from Trysull, in July 1918. This large gap would indicate that there were more people, of whom we no longer have a record. Eighteen served on the western front, including two in both France and Germany. Four served at home, two in India and one in both France and Mesopotamia. One was in Salonika and it is not clear where the remaining two served. Only six served in an infantry regiment, which compares to fifty-nine out of the seventy-three on the war memorials. This highlights the different casualty rates between infantry and other branches of the armed forces, highlighted by Gary Sheffield.[8] The remainder served in a variety of corps,

---

7   Wombourne Parish Council Minutes, 10th July 1919.

8   Sheffield, Gary, *Forgotten Victory*, Headline Book Publishing, London, 2001, p276.

eleven in the Royal Garrison Artillery or the Royal Field Artillery, five in the Royal Army Service Corps, two in the Labour Corps, one in the Royal Army Medical Corps and one in a Training Reserve Brigade.

Just over half, fifteen out of twenty-eight, spent time in hospital according to their military records: eight of whom were due to disease or accident. Five were discharged as 'physically unfit for duty' by military doctors and two were wounded; looking at their stories highlights the on-going effects of the war.

Private Charles Thomas, a private in the South Staffordshire Regiment, enlisted at the age of thirty-seven in January 1915 when his physical development was described as 'good': as a bricklayer's labourer, he would have been used to outdoor physical labour. He was in France in July 1915, was invalided back to the UK and discharged in June 1916, when he was granted a pension of 12s 6d a week for life, indicating that his physical incapacity was viewed as permanent. Alfred Guest was wounded in April 1917 and assessed as 30% disabled in November 1919 when he was awarded a pension of 12s a week, to be re-assessed in thirty-nine weeks. There is no information on whether this pension was extended. Harold Millward was demobilised in April 1919, when he was assessed as 30% disabled due to malaria and dysentery and was granted a weekly pension of 3s, again to be reviewed after twenty-six weeks. George Thomas from Bobbington must have been seriously disabled because his military record states he was to be permanently excluded from further medical assessment. However, his pension of 22s a week was to be reviewed after the standard twenty-six weeks.

Some people spent multiple periods in hospital; Gunner Walter Edwin Crook was one. He enlisted in April 1912 and was demobbed in October 1919 and his experiences covered nearly all the reasons a soldier might end up in hospital. He was hospitalised twice with gonorrhoea, in October 1914 and February 1916 and was returned to Britain in August 1915 with 'N Y D Mental'. He was treated in April 1916 for a 'lacerated terminal phalanx on the index finger of left hand', noted as 'trivial' and not incurred in the 'performance of military duty'. Finally, he appeared to have two spells in hospital in 1918, but the causes are not legible. Gonorrhoea was a problem with all armies from medieval times onwards, when it was first officially recognised in Western Europe. By the First World War treatment was usually successful with modern drugs. 'N Y D Mental' or 'Not Yet Diagnosed Mental Breakdown', was a more recent phenomenon; Gunner Cook was evidently suffering from shell shock, which was becoming an increasingly recognised condition caused by the intensity of terror experienced in modern warfare, especially from prolonged artillery bombardment. For the military authorities this was an 'ambiguous and porous' diagnosis, obviously exploitable as an exit ticket from the front line by those who were labelled as 'Dirty sneaks and blameworthy weaklings'. Whilst diagnosis was slowly gathering official recognition, how to treat the condition was less easily developed, resulting in many men being invalided out of the army and drawing a pension for life. In order to reduce this flow of men, the designation 'N Y D' was created, meaning that whilst signs of shell shock were visible, it had not been officially medically diagnosed, thus creating some time where the man's nerves could recover, at least to the extent that he did not have to be invalided out of the army and could still be of some use to the war effort.[9]

---

9   Barham, Peter, *Forgotten Lunatics Of The Great War*, Yale University Press, New Haven and London, 2007, p.18.

Four of the twenty-eight had at least one disciplinary charge on their record but only one for serious infringements prior to the armistice; William Herbert Ison, who had enlisted in August 1914, was serving in France when his first charges were recorded in early 1916 for 'missing from post, lying to NCO and being improperly dressed'. Then in July 1916, he is charged with 'AWOL, drunkenness and striking his superior officer whilst in the execution of his duty'. The gravity of these charges was reflected in the sentence of nine months' imprisonment with hard labour. At a review hearing, this was commuted to three months' Field Punishment One, meaning he was publicly and physically punished, which might entail being tied to a post or to wear chains whilst marching. Regulations stipulated that the punishment be applied for a specified number of hours every day, for example two hours in the morning and two in the afternoon. Field Punishment One was notorious because of the leeway allowed to local officers in it application; examples were published of soldiers being virtually suspended by their arms and ropes being applied around their necks. Ison completed his sentence in October but by November , he was again AWOL and using insubordinate language to his superior officer. This time his sentence of a year's imprisonment with hard labour was commuted to three months and transference to the 1ˢᵗ Battalion Rifle Brigade. He was released from prison in February 1917 and duly transferred. In the Rifle Brigade he was promoted to Lance Corporal on 17ᵗʰ June and there were no more charges.

Whilst William's conduct before the Armistice appears to be exceptional, after it such charges became more common. Private Harry Rogers enlisted in November 1916 and served in the RASC as a saddler; from November 1918 to December 1919, when he was demobilised, he had five charges, mainly for being drunk and absent from camp. Private Joseph Cox who had one charge before the armistice, had two more charges for general insubordination May and July of 1919 before he was demobilised. Private Thomas Burns, also in the RASC, in a motor transport repair unit from August 1914 to March 1919, had one pre-Armistice charge for not reporting a broken spring in an ambulance; after the Armistice he was charged with being AWOL for five days.

THE WAR MEMORIALS

From early on in the war, there was an effort to remember on a daily basis those who were serving in the armed forces. In August 1914, the armed forces Chaplain-General asked that each day at noon 'We should all lift up our hearts and prayers to God for a few moments on behalf of our brave Sailors, Soldiers and Airmen, wherever they may be throughout the world.'[10] Reverend Langley of St Benedict Biscop, posted a complete list of all who had joined the forces by the church entrance and arranged for the church bell to be rung daily at noon, to encourage everyone in the parish to 'Put up a prayer for all, especially from this parish, who have enlisted.'[11] At Bobbington's Holy Cross, special services were held on the third and fourth anniversaries of the outbreak of war, in August 1917 and again in 1918. The Reverend Norman Munro held 'Special Services of Humble Prayer to Almighty God on behalf of the Nation and Empire in this time of war' on the first Sunday of 1915 and 1916.

The news of the Armistice on 18th November 1918 came through too unexpectedly to be celebrated by a service in any of

10 Bilton, David, *The Home Front In The Great War : Aspects Of The Conflict 1914 – 1918*, Pen & Sword Books, Barnsley, 2003, p17.

11 D5841/7/1 – Vestry Minutes St Benedict Biscop 8th April 1915: Staffordshire Archives.

the churches. Nor was the signing of the Versailles Peace Treaty on 28th June 1919 celebrated in the churches but all of them held special services on Sunday 6th July, which was officially designated as a 'Day of Thanksgiving' for the signing of the peace treaty. Only the St Benedict Biscop Register of Services records an official church service for the Peace Celebration on 19th July 1919; it is possible that each church made its own individual arrangements for marking these key events. The Reverend Norman Munro at Holy Cross in Bobbington, held services from 1st to 4th July 1919, marked in his Register of Services in red ink rather than the usual black. He used his register to record somewhat more than the bare details of services and in December 1916 he noted 'End of 1916 and the second year of the great killing. Thomas Morris of White Cross was killed at the Dardanelles and George Thomas of Crab Lane and William Gardiner of Bobbington were wounded – both in France.' In these few words we have the impression of a man of compassion, affected by the events of the war.[12]

Each community wanted to mark their service losses in a more permanent fashion and prominent position, usually by a plaque, column, statue or a public space. Trysull appears to be the first in Smestow Vale to complete the task on Sunday 28th December 1919.[13] The special service of 'Dedication of churchyard cross and tablet – War Memorials' was led by the Reverend Andrews and Lionel Payne Crawfurd, Bishop of Stafford.[14] St Benedict Biscop in Wombourne unveiled their memorial on Sunday 25th

12 D5841/2/1 - Wombourne St Benedict Register of Services; D3452/2/4 – Trysull All Saints Register of Services; D5148/2/1 – Bobbington Holy Cross Regsiter of Services; D7093/1/7 – Himley St Michael Register of Services: Staffordshire Archives.

13 D3452/2/4 - Trysull All Saints Register of Services: Staffordshire Archives.

14 In the Register of Services Lionel Crawfurd is known as Lionel Stafford, reflecting his position of Bishop of Stafford.

The unveiling of Wombourne's memorial on Sunday 25th April 1920 was very well attended, as this photograph of the event shows. There was a desire to ensure that the sacrifices would not be forgotten.

April 1920, again, with a special service led by Bishop Lionel Crawfurd. Both crosses were placed in the church grounds and were easily visible from the road. There is no record of how they were paid for, but a Wombourne War Memorial Fund of £2 4s 9d was declared at a Vestry meeting in 1927, so presumably various fundraising and subscription activities had taken place over the previous seven or eight years.[15]

In March 1919, Swindon Parish Council decided that 'A public parish meeting be held on 8th April 1919, to consider the form of a memorial to soldiers who have fallen and suffered in the war. Also for those who have returned. The Reverend Charleton Chinner to be asked to chair the meeting'. The resulting window

---

15 D5841/6/1 - Wombourne St Benedict Vestry Notices and Orders: Staffordshire Archives.

was dedicated on the 12th August 1923 at the evensong service, led by the Reverend Cecil Holroyd Baker; the sermon was delivered by the Reverend T. G. Swindell, vicar of Sedgley.

At Bobbington's Vestry meeting in January 1921, the chief business was to approve that "The memorial tablet with design and inscription as entered recording the loss of Private Thomas Morris in the Great War be approved and that a petition be forwarded to the diocese requesting for the granting of a faculty to legally authorise its erection and fixing on the internal wall of the parish church of Bobbington."[16] In October 1921, Himley also discussed the erection of a plaque in the church and permission from the diocese was granted in January 1923 for a 'tablet of oak with an inscription in the chancel'.[17] The £21 cost was to be covered by subscriptions.[18]

---

16 D5148/3/1 - Bobbington Holy Cross Parish Book: Staffordshire Archives.

17 D5993/2/2/1 - Himley St Michael Parochial Church Council: Staffordshire Archives.

18 D599/2/1/6 – Himley St Michael War Memorial: Staffordshire Archives.

The Home Front

BURIALS AND DEATHS

The most obvious impact on life in the villages was the death of these seventy-three men, from a population of about 3,200. As already mentioned, the majority of these burials occurred close to the place of death, France, Gallipoli or, in the case of Ordinary Seaman Rogers, Scotland. However, burials appeared to increase in Smestow Vale. An analysis of the burial records for Wombourne shows that the average of 18.4 burials a year for the period 1st January 1910 to 30th July 1914 increased to 25.8 for the period 1st August 1914 to 1918, and then reduced to 20.3 for the period 1919 to 1922. Males accounted for the majority of these changes, their rate increased from 7.8 per annum in the pre-war years to 13.2 during the war and then fell back to 10.0 in the immediate post-war years. 1915 was the highest year with twenty-two burials but 1917 and 1918 were also relatively high. The numbers of burials of males between the ages of eighteen to forty per annum was 0.4 for the pre-war period, 1.2 for the war period and then 0.9 for the post war period. However, the average age of death across the periods varied only a little, remaining around forty-six years. There was no apparent influx of elderly migrants to the village, given that the majority of those who were buried, were living in the village in 1901. This sharp increase would certainly have added to a morbid atmosphere in the village, even if the cause of this increase remains, for this work at least, a mystery.

The deaths of men in the war would have affected the families left behind, leaving a gap where a father, husband or son would

An initial message that a loved one is missing 'in the field' was communicated by an impersonal note from the Force Record Office. This one for Private Lewis Tranter, is dated 12th July 1916. The second, dated 24th May 1917, simply states that as no further news has been received, "the Army Council have been regretfully constrained to conclude that he is dead." Wolverhampton Archive: DX-752/1.

normally have been present. Despite how sensitively it was done, the bureaucracy of managing the effects of the war would have reminded the next of kin for many years to come.

A few months after being informed of his death, the next of kin would be sent the personal belongings of the deceased; Rifleman William Henry Crook's mother received his personal belongings in February 1917, seven months after he died of wounds on 13th July 1916. They amounted to: 1 pocket wallet, postcards, 1 cig case, 1 pipe lighter, 1 ring, 1 strap, 9 buttons, 2 titles, 1 clasp knife, 1 ribbon (bar).Joseph Thomas Lawley's wife Alice, received his personal belongings in January 1919, over three months after he was killed in action in September 1918. His personal possessions were even fewer; 1 purse, letters, 1 matchbox case, 1 pair of scissors, 1 cap badge. Ernest Cresswell's possessions were returned to his mother Annie in April 1918, six months after his death in November 1917, in the Second Battle of Passchendaele. They consisted of letters, a book, discs and 3 souvenir brooches. After this, in the early 1920s, the various medals each serving man was entitled to were distributed and their receipt had to be acknowledged. Alice Crook did so on 10th April 1921, Annie Cresswell on 3rd October 1921 and Alice Lawley on 9th May 1922.

Some families would have felt the losses more than most for a variety of reasons, especially when they suffered more than one death. Thomas and Nellie Hale lost two of their four children, Leonard and Cecil; whilst William and Sarah Nicholls also lost two of their six sons. Jane Guest of Rookery Lane, who had lost her husband Benjamin in 1889 aged only thirty-nine, then lost two of her sons in November 1914 and April 1919. Similarly, James Rogers of Lower End, lost his wife Alice before 1911 and then lost his eldest son John, in 1917.

Perhaps the most tragic losses occurred to Alice Saunders, whose first husband William had died before the war. During the war she lost her eldest son Alfred William Saunders from this her first marriage in 1917, followed by her second husband, Joseph Thomas Lawley, in September 1918.

Military records can only give brief insights into the loss people felt when a loved one died, but a poignant moment is captured in William Henry Walker's record; it appeared that he had no immediate family still alive when he signed up on 1st November 1915, because he stated that his next of kin was his landlord, Mr Samuel Crane of Seisdon. Included in his record is a letter from Miss Marion McIntosh, stating that in his will, William Walker had left everything to her because he 'has no other living relation'. In this letter, she says 'I *was* the fiancée of Private Walker', with the '*was*' written over the original '*I am*'.

The physical impact of these losses might have been somewhat less immediate for the families involved, as there was a well-established history of the young leaving the villages, due to the stagnant nature of the local occupational structures, where agriculture, especially market gardening and its associated occupations, was the main employer, followed by the iron works in Swindon. Tertiary occupations, especially domestic service, were also important employments. Some youngsters lived in the villages but worked elsewhere; Wolverhampton, Dudley and Stourbridge are all within 7 miles, but many worked too far away to allow a daily commute, so they moved location. The locations of eighty-four of the 102 people known to have served in the war, were traced through the 1911 census. Of these thirty-one, 37% were not resident in Smestow Vale and of the fifty-three who were living in Smestow Vale, twenty-nine were under eighteen years old and a further fourteen were aged eighteen to twenty. So, predominantly, those who are recorded as being resident in Smestow Vale, are the young who have not yet taken the step of emigrating. This is confirmed by the relative average ages of the two groups; eighteen for those still in residence and twenty-two for those who had left.

All levels of Wombourne society suffered losses during the war. The Shaw-Helliers of the Wodehouse, one of the most prominent families in Smestow Vale; the Sankeys of the Bilston engineering firm of the same name and the Goodyears (not connected to the tyre business but file and tool manufacturers); the Grazebrooks, a Dudley industrialist, and the Furnisses, an electrical and mechanical engineer, all lost a son. The full range of local occupations is represented by the other deaths, with sixteen farm workers, six domestic workers, five iron foundry workers, a land agent's clerk, a tube maker, a canal boatman and a bicycle maker amongst the others.

THE PEACE CELEBRATIONS 19ᵀᴴ JULY 1919

As already noted, the government nominated that Peace Celebrations would be held on Saturday 19th July 1919 and a series of circulars was sent through County Councils asking Parish Councils to make appropriate arrangements. The circular was read out to the Wombourne Parish Council on 7th July 1919 and during the discussions it was suggested that 'The men from the parish who had served in the war' should be entertained. However, 'this was found to be impossible at the present time, owing to the food difficulty'. Instead, it was agreed to give the school children a treat and the cost (of about £25) was to be raised by voluntary contributions. However, three days later on the 10th July things had changed completely; the vicar, Reverend H. L. Langley, reported to the Parish Council that 'Mr. Shaw-Hellier was to provide a beast for a dinner for men who had served in the war'. It had been calculated that 'about 140 men' had served in the armed forces. Vegetables and refreshments were to be provided by others as voluntary contributions. Various councillors added to the contributions already promised. The Parish Council requested the clerk to ask Dudley Woodside Band to submit a tender for the day, 'to be accepted if it was reasonable'. A treat for the children would be a tea by Mrs Walker, a local shopkeeper. Finally, the Parish Council decided a public meeting would be called on 14th July, to inform the residents of what had been organised.[19] Swindon Parish Council's meeting was the day after Wombourne's on the 8th July, where the same circular was read and it was agreed that a meeting should be held on the following day to discuss the Peace Celebrations. Similar to Wombourne, it was agreed that cold sandwiches and tea be given to all Swindon children under the age of fifteen and a hot dinner to all returned soldiers in the parish. In addition, all old people in the parish were to be invited to the tea, prizes were to be given to the young people for sports, and if funds allowed, entertainments would be provided for the women and the parishioners in general. Local people and businesses were to be asked for donations.[20] Unfortunately, we have no records of what the other parishes did; Trysull and Seisdon Parish Council met on 1st July but do not appear to have discussed the matter. Perhaps they had not received the circular and something was organised on a more informal basis.

Neither do we have information on the actual celebrations themselves. However, it was reported to the Wombourne Parish Council in October 1919 that there was 'a balance of £6 on the Peace Celebration account', which presumably means that the voluntary contributions more than covered all the costs (no mention was made of what to do with this money). On 25th September, Swindon Parish Council reported a 'Meeting to be organised with Reverend C. Chinner to discuss what to do with the surplus funds after the Peace Celebrations'. In October, it was reported back to the council that 'an illuminated address

---

19 Wombourne Parish Council Minutes.

20 D5736/1 – Swindon Parish Council Minutes 16th April 1896 To 26th July 1948: Staffordshire Archives.

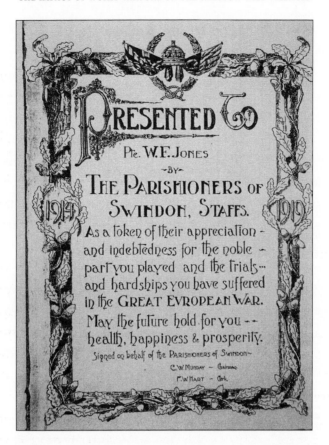

The 'Illuminated Address' the Reverend Chinner was asked to present to
the returned soldiers by Swindon Parish Council. Thanks to May Griffiths
for this image.

be given to each returned soldier and to the next of kin of those
who had fallen.' At the next month's meeting, Councillor Ashlee
produced the illuminated address, stating that the cost was £31
12s 7d. Though most of this would be covered by the balance
from the Peace Celebrations of £26 1s 8d, it was decided to hold
a dance in the school and ask the Peace Celebration Committee
to assist the Parish Council in their efforts to clear the balance.

Demobilisation And Veterans' Organisations

At a national level, the demobilisation process took some time, with approximately 3.8 million men in the army in November 1918. By November 1919 this was down to 0.9 million but pre-war levels were not reached until 1922. Along with commitments emanating from the Versailles Treaty, there were also problems enforcing the terms of the treaty on a reluctant Germany. Additionally, there were still troop commitments in Russia and in other parts of central and Eastern Europe, all of which required the maintenance of a sizeable British army in Europe until 1921. The national experience is reflected in the demob dates of the Smestow Vale men. The first person recorded as demobilised after the war was Private Charles Frederick Fazey on the 26th February 1919. Five were demobbed in March 1919 and four in April 1919, then a steady release took place from September 1919 until the end of March in 1920, when the last person was demobilised. Not everything went smoothly, as Gunner William H. Rogers found out when he discovered on 23rd August 1919 that he was not technically demobilised, even though he had been working for the London and North Western Railway since the previous March. This came to light because his new employer wanted to see his discharge papers before officially converting his employment from temporary to permanent and the records officer stated that he had not been given permission to issue them. The discharge notice was finally issued on 16th December 1919, almost four months after the problem came to light.

Veterans' associations, such as that for the 6th battalion of the South Staffordshire Regiment were active. On 27th April 1920, it was announced that there would be a 'grand re-union concert' at the Drill Hall on 6th May. However, the motivation for the concert may not have been entirely to support the veterans, as there was also a comment that a 'meeting of old soldiers should have an inspiring influence on recruits'. Organisational problems were highlighted, noting that it was proving difficult to find the addresses of many of the men and therefore invites could not be directly sent to them.

Some other veteran organisations were of a more radical nature; it was reported in April that a 'Large number of ex-service men, councillors and others' gathered at the Manley Arms on the Wednesfield Road for the inauguration of the 'Heath Town post of the Comrades of the Great War'. Comrade Elsted was elected Captain Commandant; comrade G. F. Emery was secretary and comrade C. Griffin was treasurer, whilst comrades W. J. Jackson, W. Banks and T. Mason were elected members of the committee. Comrade J. B. Owens, who was 'Commandant Number 1 of the Wolverhampton post', congratulated the 'Heath Town Veterans upon their enterprise' and predicted that 'in a few months' time, their muster roll would show 100, whereupon the post would automatically become a branch'.

THE SMESTOW VALE VILLAGES 1914 TO 1920

Probably the most well-known impact of the war on Wombourne concerned the building of the railway line from Wolverhampton to Kingswinford. Begun in 1913, Perry and Co. had established a yard or depot at Planks Lane, where the blacksmith, carpenters, workshops and engine shed were based. Building the line employed over two hundred people in total, many of them local men and boys and would have provided a very welcome boost to local employment prospects. Parts of the line, especially the earthworks, bridges and embankments were still being built in 1915 but the growing shortage of materials and men meant that work eventually stopped and did not resume until after the war.[21]

The issues facing the Parish Councils in 1914 reflected their pre-war concerns; Wombourne was trying to persuade the Post Office to provide a telephone service to the village and the clerk Horace Sadler, was regularly requested to write to the Wolverhampton Postmaster about the desirability of these facilities for their residents. Swindon council was concerned about footpaths in the parish, particularly those linking Swindon to Wombourne across the Smestow Brook. At Wombourne's meeting in September 1914, the adoption of a housing scheme was discussed with Councillor William Cartwright declaring that 'About 12 houses were required at a rental from 3s 6d to 4s per week'; after a long discussion the general opinion was 'That no steps be taken in the matter at the present time'.

The first recorded impact of the war in the Wombourne council minutes is in January 1915, when Mr. Wells of Hazlemere Garage, Kingswinford, who provided a bus service to Wombourne, was asked to attend the meeting to answer questions about the service. When asked if he would re-instate all the buses running through Wombourne and collect parcels, he replied that 'He would not be able to run all through the village owing to the government having taken two of his buses and he expected they would require more.' He continued that 'When the war is over he will run some through the village.' 'At present they went as far as Wombourne Common on Saturday and Sunday but owing to the construction of the railway bridge, the road was in a very bad condition for motor traffic.' He said that currently, nineteen buses ran through Wombourne on Saturday, sixteen on Sunday and eleven on other days. Until the war

---

21 Williams, Ned, *By Rail To Wombourne,* Upalia Press, Wolverhampton, pp20-24.

was over, buses would stop at the bottom of Gilbert Lane, where it was proposed that a waiting room should be built and a boy employed to collect parcels and deliver them if there was time.

After this, there were no more war mentions at Wombourne meetings until July 1915, when the chairman Councillor Arthur Jenks, read a letter from the Earl of Dartmouth, Lord Lieutenant of Staffordshire asking that Wombourne arrange a 'Public Meeting... on Wednesday 4th August 1915, the anniversary of the commencement of the war' for the National Patriotics Organisation. It was 'Unanimously decided to arrange a meeting on that date in the schools at 8pm.' The Central Committee For National Patriotic Organisations (CCNPO) was a propaganda organisation, established by Henry Cust at the outbreak of the war, to boost morale and encourage enlistment by publishing posters and pamphlets, supplying articles to the press and organising public meetings and lectures. The Committee organised tours using specially equipped caravans, which they called "War Vans"; it was one of these tours that the Earl of Dartmouth wanted Wombourne Parish to promote. Although the CCNPO had support from politicians at all levels, including the Prime Minister Herbert Asquith and Arthur Balfour, they were not an officially recognised government organisation.[22] Presumably this letter was the same one sent to Trysull and Seisdon, also on 22nd July 1915 though their report and response was slightly different; their minutes record that they were being asked by the Lord Lieutenant to consider a 'Parish Patriotic Meeting', which they decided to hold on 4th August and they would 'try to get some speakers to address the meeting'.[23]

---

22 http://www.lincstothepast.com/Records-of-the-CCNPO--Central-Committee-for-National-Patriotic-Organisations-/900215.record?pt=S.

23 D6339/1/1 - Trysull And Seisdon Parish Council Minutes: Staffordshire Archive.

FOOD

Food production often featured in the Wombourne minutes. In November 1915 it was agreed, as requested by the County Council, that there should be a public meeting, to be held in the schools on Thursday December 9th, in connection with Lord Selbourne's scheme 'To organise the supply of agricultural labour and production of food within the county'. On 3rd March 1916, the chairman Arthur Jenks, said he had 'Received several circulars suggesting a canvass of women for workers on the land'. The minutes report that 'several members took part in the discussion which followed, but no action was taken.' Food production was slowly being organised to deal with war-time conditions. Ten months later in January 1917, Mr Jenks informed the council about a written report 'of the War Agricultural Committee in reference to uncultivated land.' Further, the Board of Agriculture and Fisheries (through Staffordshire County Council) requested information on the 'quantities of Seed Potatoes…required in each parish, to arrange for their distribution, and to collect cash with orders'. After another long discussion the clerk was 'instructed to have notices distributed in the parish inviting applications from garden and allotment holders who required small quantities of seed potatoes'. Meanwhile, Swindon Parish Council decided at their meeting in January 1917, to write to the landlords "Marsh" and "Hill" requesting that 'their tenants, Bytheway, Gregory and Rew (or Kew?) be asked to cultivate their land or find other tenants to do so'.[24]

As 1917 progressed, food production became a more critical issue, to the extent that even the food lost to vermin was being investigated. In May, Seisdon Rural District Council asked all

---

24 D5736/1 – Swindon Parish Council Minutes 16th April 1896 To 26th July 1948, 30th January 1917: Staffordshire Archives.

Parish Councils to set up 'Rat and Sparrow Clubs'. To encourage people to destroy these pests by the payment of a bounty: 1s per dozen rat's tails; 3d per dozen heads of fully fledged house sparrows; 2d per dozen heads of unfledged house sparrows and 1d per dozen of house sparrow eggs. Wombourne decided they would be the committee of the club and Mr Sadler, the parish clerk, would act as secretary. Swindon decided to put a notice up at the Post Office and in Smestow Chapel. Trysull and Seisdon took a less active approach; 'After considerable debate the clerk was instructed to write to the different farmers in the parish asking them to take this matter into their own hands'.

Local initiatives to boost food production were also considered in the summer of 1917; at the Wombourne meeting, Mr. Apse suggested 'forming an Association for allotment holders'; more information was requested but no decision was made. In September, Swindon decided to arrange a parish meeting to discuss a scheme for forming a "Food Production Club" and at a meeting in December, Mr Clewley, the Seisdon Rural District representative, explained to Wombourne that if they formed a Food Production Society, it would assist production by coordinating 'Purchasing seeds and fertilizers'. A public meeting to form this Society was duly arranged for Thursday 20th December.

By the spring of 1918, food supply was becoming a major problem in Swindon and the Parish Council wrote to 'The Food Controller in Lichfield Street, Wolverhampton regarding the scarcity of meat in Swindon Parish'. Given the rural character of much of Swindon, conditions must have been hard if they were short of meat. The Controller replied that the 'supply of meat to Swindon will be by Moses Fox of Wombourne'.

In March 1918 the subject of allotments was raised again but little progress appears to have been made since it was last discussed the previous August. This time, Wombourne Council was appointed as the agent of the 'County War Agricultural Executive Committee to arrange rents etc'. Land had been identified at Wombourne Common and the occupier, Mr. C. W. Munday, wanted '£3 per acre rent, plus the rates, and to pay him the government price for ploughing'. The council decided to offer '£2 per acre including rates, and the ploughing to be arranged later'. In April it was noted that Mr. Munday still wanted £3 per acre plus rates, but he would do the ploughing for free. Arthur Jenks said he would meet Mr. Munday to see if he could 'come to some arrangement with him.'

AIR RAID PRECAUTIONS

Air raids by bombers on the Channel ports first occurred in December 1914 and an air campaign began on the night of 19th/20th January 1915 with Zeppelins and Schutte-Lanz airships, which continued throughout the war, though by 1917, they were largely carried out by airplanes. The initial attacks caused widespread alarm but little military or civilian damage but as the war progressed, both deaths and damage increased. Mr Jenks, the warden of St Benedict Biscop, reported that he had 'Insured the church for an extra sum of £9 against Zeppelin raids'; this was a substantial increase in the running costs of the building.[25] There was a lack of government and local authority preparation for air defence which took some time to be fully addressed. At their April 1915 meeting, Trysull and Seisdon Council discussed the fire hose and a 'night was fixed to try it'.[26] In March 1916,

25 D5841/7/1 – Vestry Minutes St Benedict Biscop, 18th May 1916: Staffordshire Archives.

26 D6339/1/1 - Trysull And Seisdon Parish Council Minutes: Staffordshire Archives.

the Superintendent of Police and the clerk to Seisdon Rural District Council wrote to Wombourne and Swindon, asking that they make immediate arrangements to inform their parishes 'as quickly as possible' of the approach of hostile aircraft, 'to enable the inhabitants to seek places of safety, or cover, until the raid is over.' Wombourne agreed to ask for the hooter at the Perry and Co. yard to be sounded as the signal. Swindon decided to write to Mr Ludlow, the manager at the ironworks, to ask Messrs Baldwin 'to receive information from the Police authorities at Tettenhall, as to the approach of hostile aircraft, on their private telephone at the works'. For Swindon residents, 'the hooter at the works' was to be used and the works was also asked to darken their windows', presumably an early form of blackout. The Bratch Water Works was to be asked for the keys of 'hydrants in case of fire', a hose should be purchased for the hydrants and the manual fire engine from Messrs Baldwins' Works was to be borrowed if necessary.[27] Trysull and Seisdon reported that 'Mrs Mander had kindly offered the use of her motor car' and made a list of people who might be able to help if required, they also nominated Mr McLachlan as a 'special messenger to Penn to warn police'.[28]

WINTER FUEL

In the summer of 1917 the issue of winter fuel for the parishes, particularly the poor, was discussed. Wombourne decided to purchase fifty tons of coal, at an estimated cost of £70, to be stored at the vicar's coach-house; Swindon also decided to buy two hundred tons, (a substantially larger amount per resident than

27 D5736/1 – Swindon Parish Council Minutes 16th April 1896 To 26th July 1948, 3rd March 1916: Staffordshire Archives.

28 D6339/1/1 - Trysull And Seisdon Parish Council Minutes: Staffordshire Archives.

Wombourne) and a Mrs Piper was to be asked if she would store it. In December, Wombourne's clerk Horace Sadler, borrowed scales to measure the coal, for sales on Tuesdays and Fridays from 2:00pm to 4:00pm, beginning on Tuesday 18th. These were discontinued in March 1918 because 'demand was very small' and it was noted that twenty-eight tons, 15.5cwt still remained, a little over half of the original quantity. To cover costs, this would have to be sold at 31s per ton, a significant premium over the retail price. The vicar offered to take ten tons, various others took another eleven and the remainder would be sold to the general public. Bobbington ran a similar scheme, and their records give an indication of price inflation over the four years, from 16s 6d in 1913 to 19s 6d in 1918.[29]

HOUSING

At the Wombourne meeting in September 1917, the question of 'Housing for working classes' was raised by letters from the Local Government Board and Seisdon Rural District Council. Parish Councils were asked to report the number of new houses currently required and the number they estimated should be built at the close of the war, 'To provide necessary accommodation for persons of the working class', as well as how many they thought 'May reasonably be expected to be provided at the close of the war by private enterprise'. A 'long discussion' is noted in the minutes and 'Councillor Jones proposed and Councillor Passmore seconded, that twenty additional houses were required, twelve at Wombourne and eight at Wombourne Common'. It was thought 'very doubtful if any will be provided by private enterprise'. Swindon noted , with less discussion, that ten new houses were

---

29 D6679/1/1 - Bobbington Parish Council Minutes: Staffordshire Archives.

needed at once and twenty more would be needed after the war, with 'No reasonable expectations that any provision for building the same would be afforded by private enterprise'.

WAR BONDS AND FUND RAISING

Though funding the war was a major issue for the central government, with many schemes and fundraising events being held for the war effort, there is no mention of these in the Wombourne Parish Council minutes, while Swindon only refers to one such event in February 1918, when War Savings and "Tank Bank Week" were discussed, it was 'agreed to approach Messrs Baldwin for assistance in taking out war bonds in "Tank Bank Week" at Wolverhampton. Various farmers would also be written to regarding the same matter, it would be interesting to know how they responded to such a direct approach to take part in the fund raising.

THE POLICE

An interesting point is raised by two different parish councils on the role and approach of the local police officer. In September 1915 Trysull and Seisdon asked their clerk to write to the Chief Constable of Staffordshire saying that 'PC Hill is making himself obnoxious and disagreeable in the parish' and that it would be 'to the interest of the parish' if he were moved. Over the following years, Swindon parish council wrote three times to the Chief Constable saying that 'PC Scott is exceeding his duties, and showing a certain amount of animus against different parishioners'. A reply was received by Swindon parish council in May 1917 from the Deputy Chief Constable, E. W. Breton, but no further details are provided; perhaps there were conflicts of roles and responsibilities between the constables and the parish council officers, as more central control was applied to day to day living due to the pressures of the war.[30]

Ongoing Impact

Life began to return to a peacetime footing after the Armistice of November 1918 but not necessarily to pre-war conditions. The building of the railway line was re-started in 1919 but was not fully opened to the public until May 1925, mainly because of the effect of mine workings between Himley and Baggeridge Junction; a cause of some concern to Wombourne, who sent a number of letters on the matter to the Great Western Railway. They also requested that a halt be installed in Wombourne Common.[31]

The telephone service to Wombourne was discussed again at a meeting in July 1919 and the clerk was also asked to write to the 'Birmingham and Midland Motor Omnibus Company about increasing services for Wombourne on Mondays, Wednesdays and Saturdays'. It was reported that the buses arriving at Gilbert Lane from Stourbridge were generally full, and some of the buses were asked to be run into Wombourne. Trysull and Seisdon also instructed their clerk to write to the postmaster in Wolverhampton asking that arrangements for fixing the telephone to Trysull and Seisdon should be carried out as soon as possible' now that the war was over.

In the winter of 1918/19 there was another winter fuel scheme in Wombourne, with a recorded deficit of £9 5s 7d but no further mention is made of it in the minutes. Support for food growing

---

30 D5736/1 – Swindon Parish Council Minutes 16th April 1896 To 26th July 1948; D6339/1/1 - Trysull And Seisdon Parish Council Minutes: Staffordshire Archives.

31 Williams, Ned, pp 20-24.

Food production became critical for the nation as the war progressed and methods to expand local and own-grown food sources were explored.

for personal consumption continued; Wombourne Parish Council bought a Holder Harriden Sprayer, at a cost of £4 13s, whilst Trysull and Seisdon bought a cheaper version at £3 18s 6d (see image above); these were to be hired to parishioners to spray their smallholdings. The parish minutes record the continued rental of land at Wombourne Common at a cost of £6 per annum plus rates (Mr Munday must have driven a hard bargain with the chairman Mr Jenks). Other pieces of land around Planks Lane were noted as possible allotments but eventually they were all used for housing. Twenty Swindon residents requested allotments from the Parish Council and were encouraged to form a 'Food Production Society' and land was acquired to provide allotments in Swindon in 1919.

In December 1918 Swindon council wrote to H Taylor, presumably at Seisdon District Council, asking 'What is being done in regard to the housing scheme for Swindon, as we are badly in want of houses'. Working relationships between Rural and Parish councils were sometimes strained, as evidenced by Swindon council's letter in January 1919, asking 'under what conditions the new houses were to be put up on' and that 'they understood that the surveyor or architect had been over and they knew nothing of it' but 'a deputation of Swindon Parish Council would be pleased to meet him' if he was to come again. In May 1919 delegates from all parish councils were summoned to attend a meeting to hear information on the various District Council schemes for 'The housing of the working classes'. Open meetings were held across the parishes in June 1919 at which opposition to some of these plans, especially from the agent of the Earl of Dudley, who did not want to have so many houses built in Swindon, was raised. In October there was a presentation by Mr Marcus Brown, architect, and Mr A J Edwards' to the Parish Council 'on the plans for new houses in Wombourne'.

Trysull and Seisdon preferred the government inspector's recommended site for new houses on the Smestow road and also noted that the new cottages should have half an acre of garden instead of an eighth as 'this would attract a better class of tenant and encourage cottage or market gardening'. However, in February 1921, they wrote to the district council saying that 'The building of the cottages in this parish is not necessary and be abandoned'.

Conclusion

The mixture of change and continuity revealed by contemporary documents over this period is striking. The losses suffered by families changed them profoundly and the experiences of the returnees would have remained with them for the rest of their lives, sometimes physically as well as mentally. Larger social changes caused or magnified by the war across the country must have had their influence, but many aspects of rural life in Smestow Vale seemed almost unaffected. It might be reading too much into the history of a relatively small and unimportant area as this but perhaps this perception of stagnation helped to cause the general feeling after the Second World War that 'Things had to change after this war' and resulted in the Labour Party victory in July 1945.

Further Research

In the course of producing this pamphlet I came across many stories I would like to have followed up further, but unfortunately could not find the information. If anyone knows more about the following stories, or have any information they would like to share, please do contact me. I was told that in 1914, some German mining engineers were undertaking exploratory drilling in the area for potential coal seams to develop and that they had to leave quickly in July 1914. Himley Hall was used as a hospital and recuperation facility, towards the end of 1918 and the grounds were apparently also used to train a cavalry unit but no details are known. The ironworks in Swindon must have benefited from the increased demand for iron during the war but there is little information on how the works developed from 1914 to 1918. Finally, the District Council presented Trysull and Seisdon Parish Council with a 'German gun' (presumably an artillery piece handed over as part of the Armistice and peace treaty). It was decided in March 1920, to place it at the 'lower corner of the Green on the Trysull side of the King George Oak' but no one seems to know what happened to it.

Appendix 1 : Those Who Died

Name	Date Of Death	Memorial	Unit	Battle / Campaign
Private William Thomas Price	3rd Sept 1914	Trysull	2nd Btn S Staffordshire Regiment	Battle Of Mons and The Retreat August - September 1914
Corporal Fred Blewitt	20th Oct 1914	Wombourne	1st Btn S Staffordshire Regiment	Fluid Fighting October - November 1914
Private William T Haynes	30th Oct 1914	Trysull	2nd Btn S Staffordshire Regiment	Fluid Fighting October - November 1914
Private Joseph Evans	7th Nov 1914	Wombourne	1st Btn S Staffordshire Regiment	Fluid Fighting October - November 1914
Private Harry Guest	12th Nov 1914	Wombourne	2nd Btn S Staffordshire Regiment	The Battle of Nonne Bosschen
Private John Rowley	12th Nov 1914	Trysull	1st Btn S Staffordshire Regiment	The Battle of Nonne Bosschen
Captain Charles Avery Grazebrook	10th Mar 1915	Himley	1st Btn King's Royal Rifle Corps	The Battle of Neuve Chapelle
Private Sidney Wilfrid Wharton	20th Apr 1915	Trysull	2nd Btn S Staffordshire Regiment	The Battle of Neuve Chapelle
Private Thomas Cox	3rd May 1915	Wombourne	6th Btn S Staffordshire Regiment	The Second Battle of Ypres
Corporal William Piper	18th May 1915	Wombourne	2nd Btn S Staffordshire Regiment	The Battle of Festubert

Name	Date Of Death	Memorial	Unit	Battle / Campaign
Private Ernest Victor Starkey Pedley	6th Aug 1915	Trysull	11th Btn Australian Imperial Force	Gallipoli
Private Thomas Morris	6th Aug 1915	Bobbington	4th Btn Worcestershire Regiment	Gallipoli
Private Thomas Baker	8th Aug 1915	Himley	7th Btn S Staffordshire Regiment	Gallipoli
Lieutenant Arthur Joseph Bradney Shaw-Hellier	9th Aug 1915	Wombourne	7th Btn S Staffordshire Regiment	Gallipoli
Captain Sydney John Sankey	25th Sep 1915	Wombourne	6th Btn S Staffordshire Regiment	The Second Battle of Ypres
Private Cyril Eric Rogers	13th Oct 1915	Wombourne	1st Btn S Staffordshire Regiment	The Battle of Loos
Lieutenant Walter Nelson	13th Oct 1915	Trysull	6th Btn S Staffordshire Regiment	The Battle of Loos
Private John Cartwright	13th Oct 1915	Himley	6th Btn S Staffordshire Regiment	The Battle of Loos
Lieutenant Francis Nicholas Andrews	11th Oct 1915	Trysull	15th Btn Royal Irish Rifles	Trench Familiarisation and Line Holding
Private T Clinton	14th Nov 1915	Wombourne	10th Btn West Yorkshire Regiment (Prince of Wales's Own)	Trench Familiarisation and Line Holding
Gunner George Henry Malpass	25th Mar 1916	Swindon	31st Divisional Ammunition Column, Royal Field Artillery	Died of Disease
Private James Chick	29th Apr 1916	Wombourne	2nd Btn S Staffordshire Regiment	Irish Rebellion Dublin
Private Lewis John Tranter	1st Jul 1916	Wombourne	1st Btn S Staffordshire Regiment	Subsidiary attack on Gommecourt

Name	Date Of Death	Memorial	Unit	Battle / Campaign
Rifleman William Henry Crook	13th Jul 1916	Wombourne	8th Btn King's Royal Rifle Corps	Battle of Delville Wood
Sergeant Isaac Leonard Williams MM	29th Jul 1916	Swindon	2nd Btn S Staffordshire Regiment	Battle of Delville Wood
Private Joseph Bennett	30th Jul 1916	Himley	9th Btn S Staffordshire Regiment	The Battle of Pozieres
Private Joseph Nicholls	15th Aug 1916	Wombourne	2nd Btn S Staffordshire Regiment	Battle of Delville Wood
Rifleman Alfred Ernest Rogers	15th Aug 1916	Not on a memorial	7th Btn King's Royal Rifle Corps	Died of Pneumonia
Rifleman Henry Pyatt	3rd Sep 1916	Wombourne	11th Btn King's Royal Rifle Corps	Battle of Delville Wood
Corporal Charles Henry Whitney	12th Sep 1916	Trysull	30th Battery, 39th Brigade Royal Field Artillery	The Battle of Flers-Courcelette
Private William Francis Bennett	19th Sep 1916	Wombourne	2nd Btn Grenadier Guards	The Battle of Flers-Courcelette
Guardsman Leonard Yeomans	25th Sep 1916	Trysull	2nd Btn Grenadier Guards	The Battle of Flers-Courcelette
Private William Henry Walker	21st Oct 1916	Trysull	95th Coy Machine Gun Corps	No recorded action
Private Thomas Sidney Parton	23rd Oct 1916	Swindon	1st Btn Royal Warwickshire Regiment	The Battle of Le Transloy
Private George Henry Baker	13th Nov 1916	Trysull	2nd Btn S Staffordshire Regiment	The Ancre

Name	Date Of Death	Memorial	Unit	Battle / Campaign
Private John Munday	28th Jan 1917	Swindon	10th Btn East Yorkshire Regiment	Died of pneumonia
Private Frederick Williams	16th Feb 1917	Wombourne	1st Btn Royal Warwickshire Regiment	Action of Miraumont
Private John Blewitt	17th Feb 1917	Wombourne	2nd Btn S Staffordshire Regiment	Action of Miraumont
Sergeant William Jones	17th Feb 1917	Wombourne	2nd Btn S Staffordshire Regiment	Action of Miraumont
Private Ernest Lindley	11th April 1917	Wombourne	112th Coy Machine Gun Corps	First Battle of the Scarpe
Lieutenant Kevin Robert Furniss	29th Apr 1917	Trysull	23rd Sqn Royal Flying Corps	General action
Private Ernest James Massey	18th Oct 1917 (wounded 11th Apr 1917)	Wombourne	6th Btn King's Own Scottish Borderers	First Battle of the Scarpe
Driver John Gallagher MM	13th April 1917	Trysull	5th Reserve Brigade Royal Field Artillery	Battle of Vimy
Lance Corporal Alfred William Saunders	23rd Apr 1917	Wombourne	8th Btn S Staffordshire Regiment	Second Battle of the Scarpe
Private Edward Porter	24th Apr 1917	Himley	12th Btn Hampshire Regiment	Salonika
Private George Hopcutt	1st May 1917	Wombourne	2nd Btn S Staffordshire Regiment	Battle of Arleux

Name	Date Of Death	Memorial	Unit	Battle / Campaign
Private John Thomas Wharton	13th Jul 1917	Trysull	1st Btn Loyal North Lancashire Regiment	German Operation Strandfest (Beach Party)
Acting Bombardier Arthur Moody	22nd Jul 1917	Swindon	56th Siege Battery Royal Garrison Artillery	General action
Ordinary Seaman John Rogers	2nd Sep 1917	Wombourne	HMS Agincourt	Died of tuberculosis
Lance Corporal John William Vincent	10th Oct 1917	Wombourne	3rd Btn Grenadier Guards	Battle of Poelcapelle
Private Charles Eli Fox	12th Oct 1917	Wombourne	8th Btn S Staffordshire Regiment	First Battle of Passchendaele
Private William Henry Reeves	17th Oct 1917	Wombourne	4th Btn Grenadier Guards	First Battle of Passchendaele
Private William Ernest Preece	21st Oct 1917	Trysull	53rd Btn Australian Imperial Force	First Battle of Passchendaele
Private Ernest Cresswell	9th Nov 1917	Trysull	1st Btn Royal West Kent Regiment	Second Battle of Passchendaele
Corporal Walter Leonard Bowen	30th Nov 1917	Swindon	2nd Btn S Staffordshire Regiment	Cambrai
Private Thomas Nichols	14th Dec 1917	Wombourne	2nd Btn S Staffordshire Regiment	Cambrai
Private Charles Corns	15th Jan 1918 (from wounds received earlier)	Swindon	3rd Btn S Staffordshire Regiment	Discharged medically unfit 10th Jul 1916.

Name	Date Of Death	Memorial	Unit	Battle / Campaign
Private Leonard Hale	30th Jan 1918 (from wounds received earlier)	Wombourne	5th Btn Grenadier Guards	Cambrai
Private John Haynes	3rd Feb 1918	Trysull	2nd Btn S Staffordshire Regiment	No recorded action
Private William Richard Millward	21st Mar 1918	Trysull and Himley	2nd Btn S Staffordshire Regiment	The Battle Of St Quintin
Private Thomas Nicholls	24th Mar 1918	Wombourne	4th Btn S Staffordshire Regiment	First Battle Of Bapaume
Private Cecil Hale	16th Apr 1918	Wombourne	1st Btn Lincolnshire Regiment	First Battle Of Kemmel
Private Walter Henry Crook	26th Apr 1918	Wombourne	4th Btn Royal Fusiliers	Battle Of Bethune
Private Aubrey Wray	29th May 1918	Himley	1st Btn S Staffordshire Regiment	No recorded actions
Private Major Howard Goodyear	5th Sep 1918	Wombourne	7th Btn Lincolnshire Regiment	Second Battle Of Bapaume
Private Harry George Bowen	12th Sep 1918	Wombourne	1st/5th Btn Devonshire Regiment	Battle of Havrincourt
Private George Henry Hobbs	14th Sep 1918	Wombourne	2nd/20th Btn London Regiment	Battle of Havrincourt
Private Joseph Thomas Lawley	20th Sep 1918	Wombourne	1st Btn The Loyal North Lancashire Regiment	Battle of Epehy
Guardsman James Edward Hopcutt	25th Sep 1918	Wombourne	2nd Btn Coldstream Guards	Battle of Havrincourt

Name	Date Of Death	Memorial	Unit	Battle / Campaign
Private John Stevens	25th Sep 1918	Wombourne	1st Btn S Staffordshire Regiment	Saint Quintin Canal
Private James Thomas Boddison	28th Sep 1918	Wombourne	1st Btn S Staffordshire Regiment	Saint Quintin Canal
Private Alex James Piper	19th Oct 1918	Swindon	1st/6th Btn S Staffordshire Regiment	The Battle of the Selle
Private Samuel Edward Wilkes	25th Oct 1918	Himley	18th Bde Royal Field Artillery	The Final Advance in Artois
Private John William Guest	8th Apr 1919	Wombourne	Labour Corps, formerly 3rd Btn Sherwood Foresters	Possibly killed in an accident

Appendix 2 : Those Who Served And Returned

Name	Enlisted	Village	Unit	Demobbed
Gunner Walter Edwin Crook	1st Apr 1912	Wombourne	Royal Field Artillery	21st Oct 1919
Driver William Page	18th Jan 1913	Wombourne	Royal Field Artillery	1st Jul 1919
Sergeant John Rowley	18th Apr 1913	Wombourne	Royal Field Artillery	11th Apr 1919
Private Thomas Burns	7th Aug 1914	Wombourne	Royal Army Service Corps	2nd Apr 1919
Private William Herbert Ison	17th Aug 1914	Wombourne	Rifle Brigade	31st Mar 1920
Private George Thomas	8th Sep 1914	Bobbington	Kings Shropshire Light Infantry	24th Jul 1917 (unfit for service)
Private Frederick William Jones	15th Sep 1914	Swindon	Royal Army Medical Corps	
Sergeant John Vale	23rd Sep 1914	Bobbington	Royal Field Artillery	29th Jan 1919
Private Henry Harry Bennett	12th Nov 1914	Trysull	S Staffordshire Regiment	6th Mar 1919
Private Arthur Disley	11th Jan 1915	Himley	Royal Army Service Corps	2nd Mar 1919

Name	Enlisted	Village	Unit	Demobbed
Private Charles Thomas	27th Jan 1915	Wombourne	S Staffordshire Regiment	17th Jun 1916 (unfit for service)
Private Sydney Hill	18th Apr 1915	Bobbington	S Staffordshire Regiment	N/K
Private Harold Millward	31st Oct 1915	Himley	Royal Field Artillery	10th Jun 1919
Gunner William Henry Rogers	15th Nov 1915	Wombourne	Royal Garrison Artillery	About Dec 1919
Private George William Davies	24th Nov 1915	Trysull	Royal Garrison Artillery	Post Apr 1919
Sapper Henry George Gregory	11th Dec 1915	Trysull	Royal Engineers	15th Mar 1919
Private George Powell	17th Mar 1916	Himley	Royal Garrison Artillery	4th Sep 1919
Driver Harry Burke	8th Jun 1916	Trysull	Royal Engineers	10th Jul 1919
Private Edward Bullock	30th Jul 1916	Wombourne	Works Btn	12th Mar 1919
Private Frederick Day	28th Sep 1916	Wombourne	Royal Army Service Corps	12th Jul 1919
Private William Tranter	21st Oct 1916	Wombourne	N/K	N/K
Gunner Eli Passmore	2nd Nov 1916	Wombourne	Royal Garrison Artillery	29th Feb 1920
Private Alfred Guest	14th Nov 1916	Wombourne	S Staffordshire Regiment	20th Nov 1919
Private Harry Rogers	16th Nov 1916	Wombourne	Royal Army Service Corps	Post Nov 1919

Name	Enlisted	Village	Unit	Demobbed
Private Charles Frederick Fazey	24th Jan 1917	Trysull	Royal Field Artillery	26th Feb 1919
Gunner Frederick Thomas Mansell	12th Mar 1917	Wombourne	Royal Garrison Artillery	7th Feb 1920
Private Joseph Cox	23rd May 1917	Wombourne	Durham Light Infantry	Post Jul 1919
Private Alfred Charles Bindschadler	31st Jul 1918	Trysull	Royal Army Service Corps	13th Mar 1919

Acknowledgements

I would like to acknowledge the support and assistance provided to me in this work by many people, and in particular the following :

Olwen Crane, of St Michael in Himley, for opening up the church especially for me.

David Balderstone, of Wombourne URC, for opening up the church for me.

May Griffiths, for permission to use various photographs and images in her possession.

Keith Lilley, Warden at St John the Evangelist in Swindon, for the use of the extensive work he has done on those from the parish who died in World War One.

Hilary Moore, Wombourne Parish Council Clerk for access to the Wombourne Parish Council Minutes.

The staff at Staffordshire Archives for their assistance.

Friends and colleagues at Wombourne History Group.